Tell Me About

SUN, STARS & PLANETS

SERIES EDITOR: JACKIE GAFF

ILLUSTRATED BY PETER BULL
& SEBASTIAN QUIGLEY

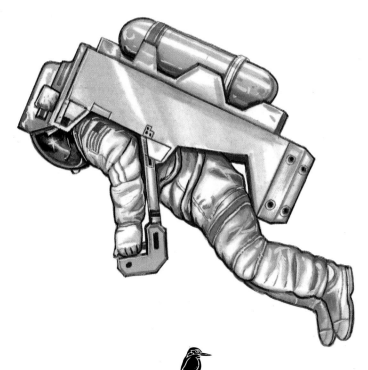

Kingfisher Books

Series editor: Jackie Gaff
Series designer: Terry Woodley
Author: Tom Stacy
Consultant: James Muirden
Designer: David West Children's Book Design
Illustrators: Peter Bull (pp. 2–3, 10–17, 20–5, 28–35);
Sebastian Quigley (pp. 4–9, 18–19, 26–7, 36–8)
Cover illustration: Ross Watton (Garden Studio)
Editor: Brigid Avison
Editorial assistant: Anne O'Daly

Kingfisher Books, Grisewood & Dempsey Ltd, Elsley House,
24–30 Great Titchfield Street, London W1P 7AD

First published in paperback in 1992 by Kingfisher Books
10 9 8 7 6 5 4 3 2 1
Originally published in hardback in 1990 by Kingfisher Books
Copyright © Grisewood & Dempsey Ltd 1990

BRITISH LIBRARY CATALOGUING IN PUBLICATION DATA
A catalogue record for this book is available from the
British Library

ISBN 0 86272 611 5

Phototypeset by Southern Positives and Negatives
(SPAN), Lingfield, Surrey
Printed and bound in Spain

Contents

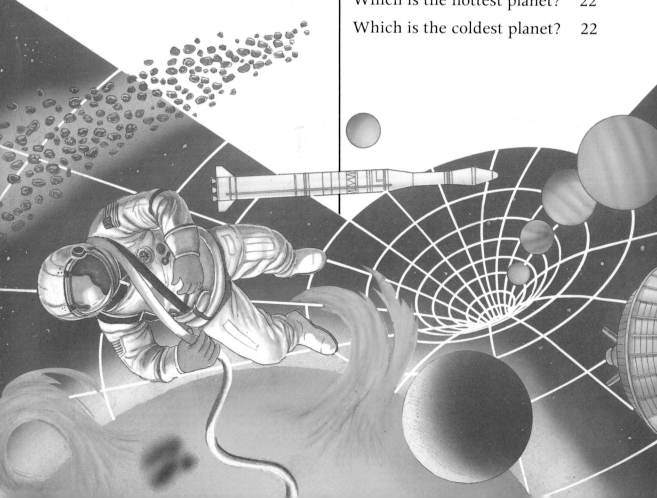

What is the Sun like?

The Sun is a star, one of the billions in Space. It is like a giant power-house – a glowing ball of hot gases, producing a vast amount of energy which streams out through Space in waves of light and heat. This energy is essential to life on Earth. Without it our planet would be too cold and dark for plants and animals to survive.

 NEVER LOOK AT THE SUN

The Sun is far too bright for our eyes. Never look directly at it, even when wearing sunglasses. Its rays are strong enough to damage your eyes or even to cause blindness.

 SUN FACTS

● The Sun is about 150 million km from the Earth.

● It is about 4.6 billion years old.

● It spins round once every 27.4 days.

● It is an average star. Some stars are thousands of times brighter, others are thousands of times fainter.

● The Sun's diameter is nearly 1.4 million km – 109 times the Earth's. One million Earths could fit inside the Sun!

● Earth

SUN

Around the Sun is a layer of gas which is called the chromo-sphere. It stretches out into Space for about 10,000 km.

Plumes of hot gas called prominences shoot thousands of kilometres into Space Some last for hours, others for days.

Sunspots are cooler areas, which look like dark blotches on the Sun's surface. They are most common every 11 or so years.

The outermost layer is a faint halo which stretches millions of kilometres into Space around the Sun. It is called the corona.

The surface of the Sun is called the photo-sphere. It looks solid, but the photosphere is really like a white-hot boiling mist.

The heat and light energy created in the Sun's fiery core can take as long as a million years to work its way through to the photosphere.

The core, or centre, of the Sun is made of a gas called helium. This is the Sun's hottest part. It is where the Sun's heat and light energy are made.

How hot is the Sun?

The Sun is far too hot to visit! The hottest part is the core, where the temperature can reach 15 million °C. Even the coolest part of the Sun, its surface, is 6000°C – at this temperature solid iron would boil away into clouds of gas! All this heat is made in the Sun's fiery heart, by a process in which hydrogen gas is changed into another gas, called helium.

 DO YOU KNOW

The Sun is always losing weight! In fact, scientists have worked out that it loses around 4 million tonnes every second – this is the amount of hydrogen gas that the Sun turns into energy every second.

 DO YOU KNOW

All substances are made of invisibly tiny atoms, which have huge amounts of energy. Some of this is given out inside the Sun, where it's so hot that hydrogen atoms break up, joining together again to form helium atoms. This is called an atomic reaction.

The Earth is surrounded by a layer of air called the atmosphere, which shields us from the Sun's burning rays.

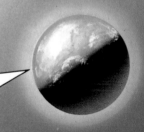

 MAKE A SUNDIAL

Push a stick into modelling clay and stand it on a sheet of paper in a sunny place. Use a ruler and pencil to mark on the paper the places where the shadow falls at different times of the day.

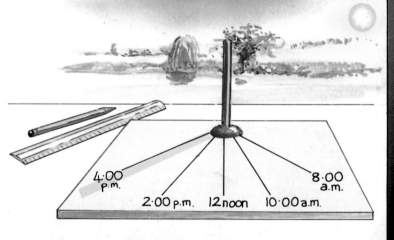

4.00 p.m. 2.00 p.m. 12 noon 10.00 a.m. 8.00 a.m.

Why does the Sun rise?

Although we can't feel it, the Earth is always moving. It orbits, or goes round, the Sun, and this journey takes a whole year. At the same time the Earth itself is spinning – one whole spin every 24 hours. As the Earth spins, the Sun comes into view and it seems to us to rise in the sky. The Earth spins from West to East, so the Sun is in the East when we first see it in the morning, and in the West when it sets in the evening.

 DO YOU KNOW

Although we can't feel it, the Earth spins at about 1600 km/h. The central line on which something spins is called an axis. The Earth's axis passes through the Poles.

Light from the Sun takes $8\frac{1}{2}$ minutes to travel 150 million km to the Earth.

We have night when our part of the Earth is turned away from the Sun's light.

From Earth, the Sun appears to travel across the sky between sunrise and sunset. But it is really the Earth that is moving, not the Sun.

How old is the Sun?

The Sun is around 4.6 billion years old. Stars are like people – they are born, live for a while, and finally die. Our Sun is an average star in size and brightness. It has now reached middle age, but in another 5 billion or so years it will have used up all its hydrogen fuel. Then it will swell to as much as 100 times its present size and become a red giant. After millions more years, this giant Sun will shrink and become a white dwarf. As it cools down, it will stop shining altogether.

 DO YOU KNOW

Light bulbs cool in much the same way as dying stars do – the filament, or wire, inside glows white, then yellow, orange, and finally red.

2 Many other stars, of different sorts, were also formed. Together, they made a cluster, or group.

1 Like all new stars, our Sun began its life in a cold dark cloud of gas and dust called a nebula.

3 Our Sun began to shine as a cool red star, as it came out of the nebula and began a life of its own.

4 The Sun will shine as a normal yellow star for most of its life. However, it may grow slightly hotter.

7 The last stage of our Sun's life will be as a white dwarf – a small but still very hot star. As it cools, it will turn yellow, orange, then red. Finally, it will slowly fade away.

9 Part of the star may survive as a neutron star. Neutron stars are small but amazingly dense. A piece the size of a pinhead would weigh as much as a house!

8 Most stars end their lives quietly as white dwarfs. But the very biggest and hottest stars, called blue giants, may blow up in a huge explosion called a supernova.

6 As they die, some stars 'leak' huge clouds of gas into Space. These clouds are called planetary nebulae.

 STAR FACTS

● The oldest stars are 15 billion years old.

● The largest stars are red supergiants. These can be 1000 times bigger than our Sun.

● The hottest stars are blue supergiants. Their surface temperature is five times hotter than our Sun's.

● The smallest stars are neutron stars, at around 15 km across.

5 Towards the end of its life, the Sun will swell to as much as 100 times its present size. It will become a red giant.

What is a black hole?

Black holes are the remains of collapsed stars. A tug of war is going on inside every star. On one side is its gravity, or pulling force, which is trying to make it collapse and become much smaller. On the other side is the energy pouring out from its core, which is trying to make it explode. For most of a star's life, its gravity and its energy balance exactly. But when the star's core runs out of fuel, its gravity wins and the star collapses. The gravity around the star is now so strong that even its own light is sucked in, making it invisible – a black hole in Space.

 DO YOU KNOW

If the Sun ever becomes a black hole, its diameter will shrink from nearly 1.4 million km to be less than 6 km.

This picture shows what would happen if a black hole and a star were close in Space – the black hole's gravity would suck in hot gases from the star.

What are shooting stars?

Shooting stars, or meteors, are the streaks of light you sometimes see at night. They are made by pea-sized bits of rock or metal called meteoroids, which fall from Space and burn up in the Earth's atmosphere.

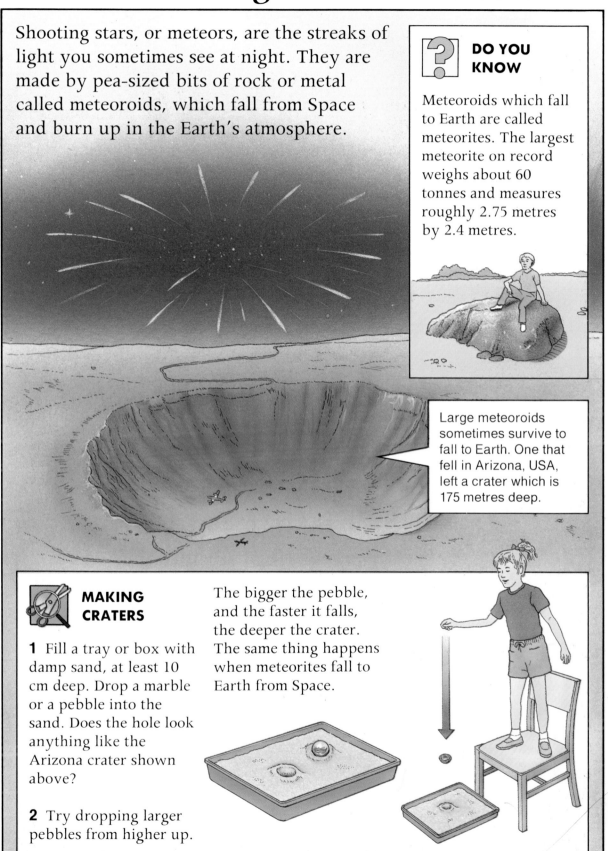

DO YOU KNOW

Meteoroids which fall to Earth are called meteorites. The largest meteorite on record weighs about 60 tonnes and measures roughly 2.75 metres by 2.4 metres.

Large meteoroids sometimes survive to fall to Earth. One that fell in Arizona, USA, left a crater which is 175 metres deep.

MAKING CRATERS

1 Fill a tray or box with damp sand, at least 10 cm deep. Drop a marble or a pebble into the sand. Does the hole look anything like the Arizona crater shown above?

2 Try dropping larger pebbles from higher up.

The bigger the pebble, and the faster it falls, the deeper the crater. The same thing happens when meteorites fall to Earth from Space.

What is Halley's Comet?

Comets are huge clouds of gas and dust, much bigger than the Earth, with a rocky core a few kilometres across. Halley's Comet is named after the English scientist Edmond Halley (1656–1742), who worked out that its orbit around the Sun brings it close to the Earth every 76 years.

In 1986 the European spacecraft Giotto passed right through Halley's Comet.

A comet's tail points away from the Sun and can be over 300 million km long.

 DO YOU KNOW

Halley's Comet was last seen in 1985-86 and it will return in 2061–62. The same comet has been seen regularly since 240 BC. It appeared in 1066 at the time of the Norman Conquest of England – it is shown as a fiery star on a scene in the Bayeux Tapestry, which tells the story of the Conquest.

Giotto was battered by comet dust, but its camera still sent pictures back to Earth.

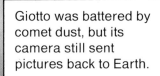

Scientists worked out that the comet's ice and rock core measured 15 km by 8 km.

Why do stars twinkle?

It is the Earth's atmosphere that makes stars twinkle. On its way to Earth, starlight passes through bands of warm and cold air in the atmosphere. These heat currents make the starlight flicker. You can see the same effect if you look at distant lights through the heat currents above a bonfire.

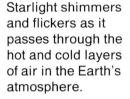

Starlight shimmers and flickers as it passes through the hot and cold layers of air in the Earth's atmosphere.

Stars only twinkle when seen from Earth. In Space they shine steadily.

STAR COMPASS

If you are in the northern hemisphere, look for the star-group called the Plough. Two of its stars point to the Pole Star – face it to look North. In the southern hemisphere, find the brightest star in the Southern Cross. Imagine a line in the sky four times as long as its longest part. Face the point at the end of this line to look to the South.

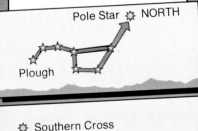

Pole Star ☼ NORTH

Plough

Southern Cross

SOUTH

What are the signs of the zodiac?

The signs of the zodiac are 12 constellations – groups of stars which make patterns in the night sky. These 12 constellations form a ring around the sky, and the planets are always somewhere in this ring. If we could see the stars in daytime, we would see that the Sun appears to move right around the zodiac in one year, spending a month or so crossing each constellation.

CONSTELLATION FACTS

● In all, 88 constellations have now been named. About half of them can be seen on any clear night. Some, such as the Great Bear, are very large. Others, such as Crux, the Cross, are very small.

● Many constellations, including the zodiac ones, were named long long ago, after animals and ancient gods and heroes.

● Although from Earth they seem to be in a group, individual stars in a constellation may be huge distances apart. Some are much farther from Earth than others.

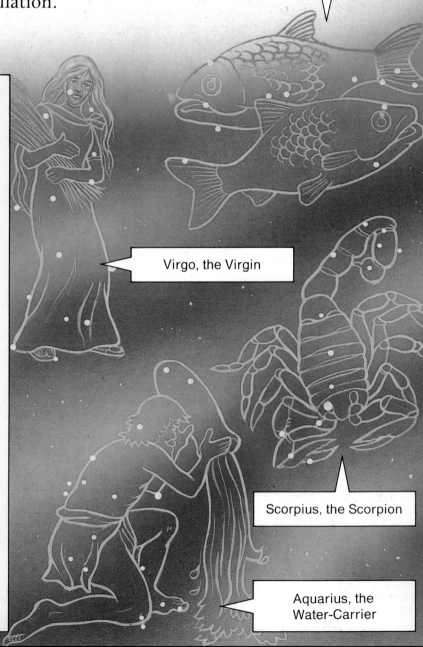

Pisces, the Fishes

Virgo, the Virgin

Scorpius, the Scorpion

Aquarius, the Water-Carrier

What do astronomers do?

Astronomers are scientists who study the stars. Before the telescope was invented in the 1600s, astronomers had to rely on their eyes alone. With this new equipment they could see much farther into Space, and they discovered other planets and millions more stars. Today, astronomers also have radio telescopes, which they use to study invisible types of energy given off by distant stars and planets.

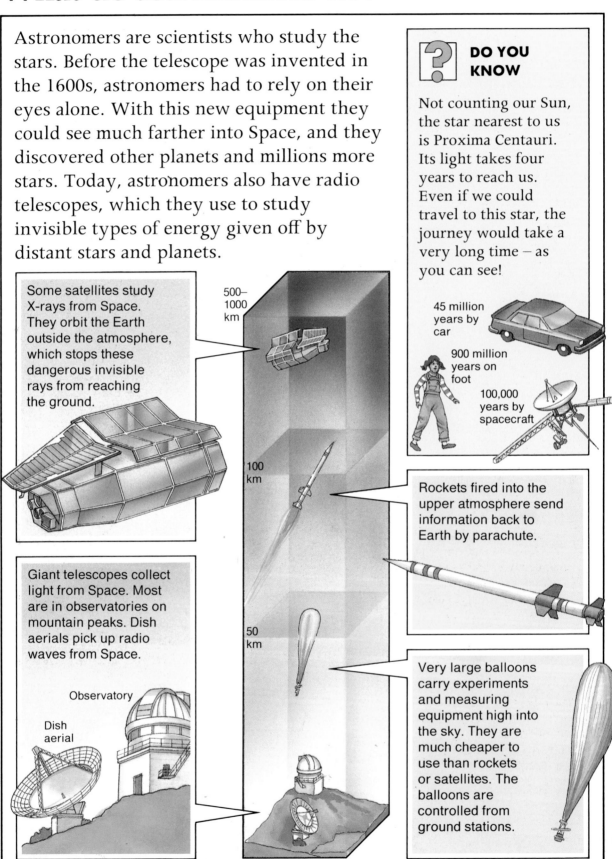

45 million years by car

900 million years on foot

100,000 years by spacecraft

Some satellites study X-rays from Space. They orbit the Earth outside the atmosphere, which stops these dangerous invisible rays from reaching the ground.

500–1000 km

100 km

Rockets fired into the upper atmosphere send information back to Earth by parachute.

Giant telescopes collect light from Space. Most are in observatories on mountain peaks. Dish aerials pick up radio waves from Space.

50 km

Observatory

Dish aerial

Very large balloons carry experiments and measuring equipment high into the sky. They are much cheaper to use than rockets or satellites. The balloons are controlled from ground stations.

What is a satellite?

A satellite is something that orbits a planet. Until the Space Age began, the Earth's only satellite was the Moon. Now it also has many artificial satellites – machines which orbit it, doing all sorts of different jobs. Some satellites relay TV and telephone signals. Some study the stars, others the Earth and its weather.

 DO YOU KNOW

To escape the Earth's gravity and go into orbit, a satellite must be boosted by a rocket to a speed of over 28,000 km/h. The first satellite, Sputnik 1, was sent up in 1957. It lasted 92 days.

Communication satellites relay TV and telephone signals. Because their orbit matches the speed at which the Earth spins in Space, they stay above the same point on its surface.

Some satellites carry special telescopes which pick up infra-red light and other light waves we can't see with our eyes. They can study young stars which aren't yet hot enough to shine.

Satellites send information down to Earth as radio signals. These are received by dish aerials at ground stations in different parts of the world.

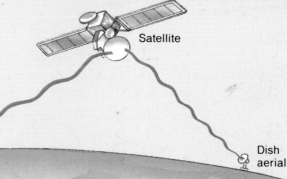

Satellite

Dish aerial

Dish aerial

What is the Milky Way?

On clear moonless nights you may have seen a fuzzy band of starlight in the sky – this is the Milky Way. It is the huge group of stars to which our Sun belongs. Star-groups like the Milky Way are called galaxies, and there are millions of them in Space. The Milky Way is a spiral-shaped galaxy – the picture here shows what it looks like from above. From the side it would look like a flat spinning dish.

GALAXY FACTS

● The Milky Way is made up of over 100 billion stars. The Sun is just one of them.

● From edge to edge, the Milky Way is about 100,000 light-years across.

● The galaxy nearest to our own is 175,000 light-years away. It is called the Large Magellanic Cloud, and it is smaller than the Milky Way.

● There are three main kinds of galaxy. Some are spiral-shaped, like the Milky Way. Others are elliptical (egg-shaped) or irregular (uneven).

STAR GAZING

On clear moonless nights, you can see lots of stars without the help of binoculars or a telescope. A planisphere is a star map which will help you to name the con-stellations you see. Dress warmly!

Planisphere

? DO YOU KNOW

Distances in Space are so great that they are measured in light-years. One light-year is 9500 billion km. This is the distance that light rays travel in a year.

This is what the three main types of galaxy look like.

From above, spiral galaxies look like giant whirlpools, with long spiralling arms of stars. The nearest spiral galaxy to ours, the Andromeda Galaxy, is more than 2 million light-years away from Earth.

Elliptical galaxies are like spiral galaxies without arms. They are thought to be made up of old and dying stars.

Irregular galaxies can be any shape. They are all smaller than the Milky Way and seem to be made of young, newly formed stars.

Our Sun (arrowed) is near the edge of the Milky Way, on a spiral arm 30,000 light-years from the centre.

What is the solar system?

The Earth is one of nine planets which orbit the Sun, and these planets and their moons make up the solar system – the word solar means 'of the Sun'. The solar system also contains thousands of minor planets, called asteroids, and countless comets. The planets, asteroids and comets are all held in their orbits by the Sun's gravity, or pulling force.

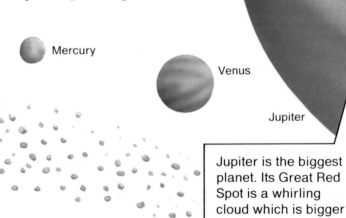

Mercury

Venus

Jupiter

DO YOU KNOW

Unlike stars, planets do not give off light. They shine at night because they reflect light from the Sun.

The planets and other objects which orbit our Sun travel in flattened circles called ellipses.

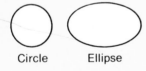

Circle   Ellipse

Jupiter is the biggest planet. Its Great Red Spot is a whirling cloud which is bigger than the Earth.

Earth

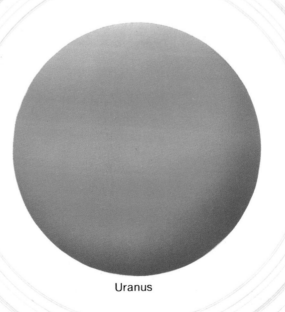

Uranus

Mars

Uranus, Jupiter, Neptune and Saturn all have rings. The rings are made of pieces of ice and dust.

PLANET FACTS

1 Mercury is the closest planet to the Sun.

2 Venus is hot, stormy and covered in cloud.

3 Earth is the only planet in the solar system with air, oceans and life.

4 Mars is a cold desert world.

About 50,000 asteroids form a belt between Mars and Jupiter.

5 Jupiter is the largest planet – all the rest could fit inside it.

6 Saturn has the brightest rings and the most moons (18 in all).

7 Uranus has 15 satellites and 13 rings.

8 Between 1979–99, Neptune's orbit makes it the outermost planet.

9 Pluto is the smallest of the planets and the least-known.

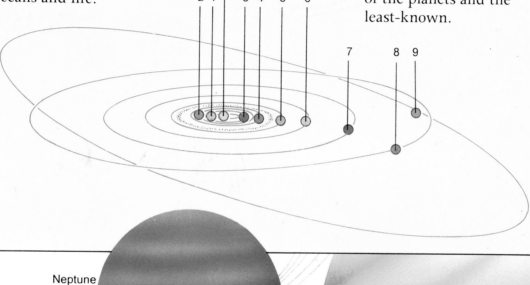

Sun

2 1   3 4   5   6   7   8   9

Neptune

Pluto

Saturn

Asteroids may be the remains of a small planet. The largest asteroid, Ceres, is about 1000 km across.

21

Which is the hottest planet?

The hottest planet is Venus, where the temperature reaches 480°C – almost five times as hot as boiling water! Venus is so hot because it is covered by thick heavy clouds of carbon dioxide gas, which trap the Sun's heat like greenhouse glass.

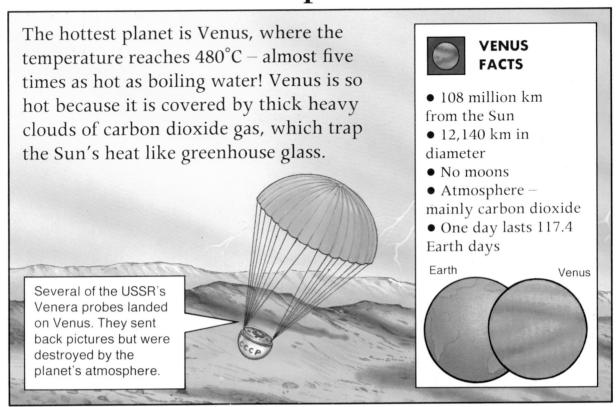

Several of the USSR's Venera probes landed on Venus. They sent back pictures but were destroyed by the planet's atmosphere.

VENUS FACTS

- 108 million km from the Sun
- 12,140 km in diameter
- No moons
- Atmosphere – mainly carbon dioxide
- One day lasts 117.4 Earth days

Earth   Venus

Which is the coldest planet?

Pluto is the coldest planet. It is so far from the Sun that hardly any warmth reaches it. The temperature on Pluto is 240°C below freezing point. The lowest recorded temperature on Earth, just below -89°C, would seem like a heatwave on Pluto!

PLUTO FACTS

- 5.9 billion km from the Sun
- 2200 km in diameter
- One moon
- Atmosphere – not known
- One day lasts 6.4 Earth days

Earth

Pluto

Which planet is nearest the Sun?

Mercury is the nearest planet to the Sun. At midday it is hotter than an oven – about 350°C. But at night it is freezing cold, because the planet has no atmosphere to keep the heat in.

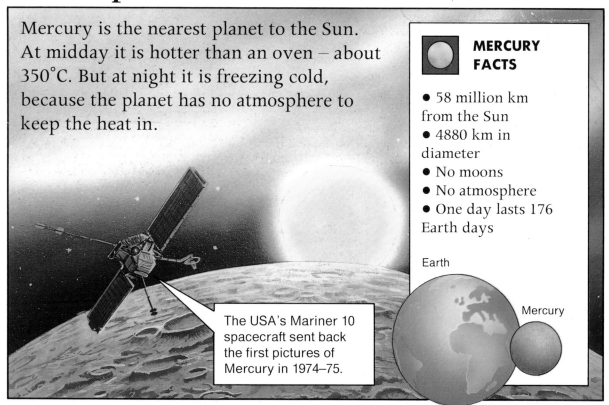

The USA's Mariner 10 spacecraft sent back the first pictures of Mercury in 1974–75.

MERCURY FACTS

- 58 million km from the Sun
- 4880 km in diameter
- No moons
- No atmosphere
- One day lasts 176 Earth days

Earth

Mercury

Which planet has the biggest moon?

The biggest planet, Jupiter, has the biggest moons in our solar system. It has 16 moons in all, and two of them are huge. Jupiter's largest moon is called Ganymede, and it is bigger than the planet Mercury. Another moon, Callisto, is nearly the same size.

Io

Europa

Callisto

Ganymede

JUPITER FACTS

- 778 million km from the Sun
- 142,800 km in diameter
- 16 moons
- Atmosphere – hydrogen and helium gases
- One day lasts nearly 10 Earth hours

Jupiter

Earth

Is there life on Mars?

Mars is the fourth planet from the Sun, and for a long time people wondered whether it was close enough to the Sun to make some form of life possible. In 1976, two US Viking spacecraft visited Mars, but they found no sign of life. Mars has very little air, no surface water, and it is bitterly cold – the temperature doesn't rise above freezing point, even in summer. Mars may once have been warmer, however. If so, it may have had water and even, perhaps, simple forms of life.

MARS FACTS

- 228 million km from the Sun
- 6790 km in diameter
- 2 moons
- Atmosphere – carbon dioxide gas
- One day lasts about 24.5 Earth hours

Earth

Mars

The rocks on Mars contain iron which has rusted – that's why the planet looks red. Wind-blown dust makes the sky look pink.

The Viking's antenna beamed signals back to Earth over 78 million km away.

A weather detector showed that Mars has dust storms and very frosty nights.

Cameras gave people on Earth their first close-up look at the surface of Mars.

A robot scoop dug up samples of soil. Tests found no sign of life, not even bacteria.

? DO YOU KNOW

About 100 years ago some astronomers said they could see what looked like canals on the surface of Mars. People wondered whether some intelligent life form had built them.

A small rocket motor slowed the spacecraft as it descended from Space to Mars.

What is Neptune like?

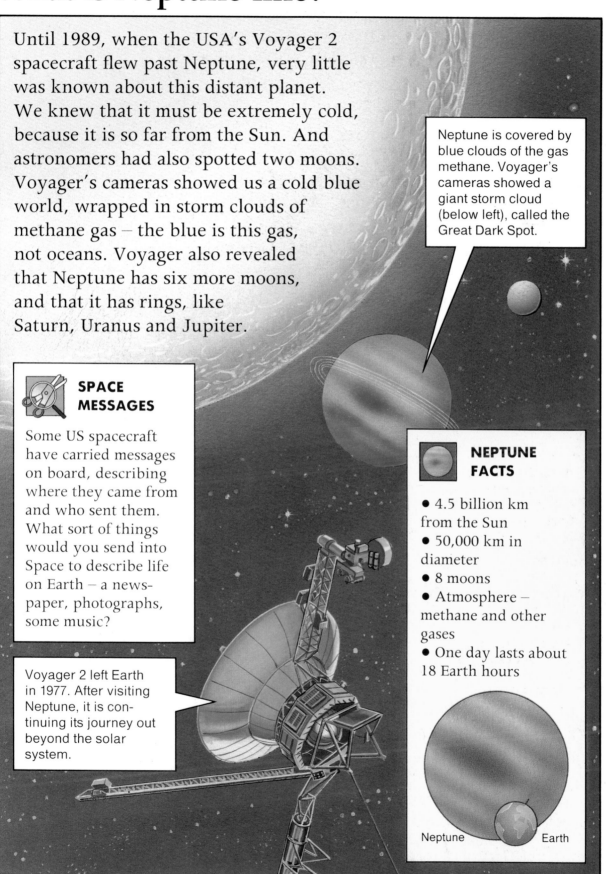

Until 1989, when the USA's Voyager 2 spacecraft flew past Neptune, very little was known about this distant planet. We knew that it must be extremely cold, because it is so far from the Sun. And astronomers had also spotted two moons. Voyager's cameras showed us a cold blue world, wrapped in storm clouds of methane gas – the blue is this gas, not oceans. Voyager also revealed that Neptune has six more moons, and that it has rings, like Saturn, Uranus and Jupiter.

Neptune is covered by blue clouds of the gas methane. Voyager's cameras showed a giant storm cloud (below left), called the Great Dark Spot.

SPACE MESSAGES

Some US spacecraft have carried messages on board, describing where they came from and who sent them. What sort of things would you send into Space to describe life on Earth – a news-paper, photographs, some music?

Voyager 2 left Earth in 1977. After visiting Neptune, it is con-tinuing its journey out beyond the solar system.

NEPTUNE FACTS

- 4.5 billion km from the Sun
- 50,000 km in diameter
- 8 moons
- Atmosphere – methane and other gases
- One day lasts about 18 Earth hours

Neptune   Earth

Who first landed on the Moon?

In 1959 a Soviet spacecraft, Luna 2, crash-landed on the Moon. Two years later, the Americans began planning a spacecraft that could carry astronauts to the Moon and back. By 1969 they were ready. Three astronauts travelled to the Moon in the Apollo 11 spacecraft, which was launched from Earth by a giant Saturn rocket. The main spacecraft orbited the Moon, while astronauts Neil Armstrong and Edwin Aldrin flew down in a small landing craft. They set foot on the Moon on 20 July 1969.

 MOON FACTS

- 384,400 km from the Earth
- 3476 km in diameter
- Atmosphere – none
- One day lasts 29.5 Earth days

- It can be as hot as 100°C and as cold as -170°C.

- It's roughly as wide as Australia.

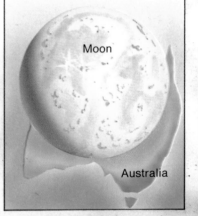

Moon

Australia

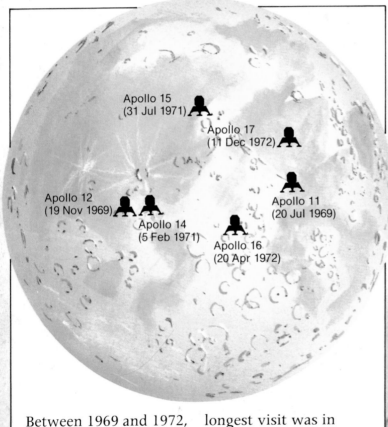

Apollo 15
(31 Jul 1971)

Apollo 17
(11 Dec 1972)

Apollo 12
(19 Nov 1969)

Apollo 14
(5 Feb 1971)

Apollo 11
(20 Jul 1969)

Apollo 16
(20 Apr 1972)

Between 1969 and 1972, six of the USA's Apollo spacecraft landed on the Moon, and 12 astronauts explored different parts of its surface. The longest visit was in December 1972, when the Apollo 17 astronauts Eugene Cernan and Harrison Schmitt stayed for almost 75 hours.

HOW FAR IS THE MOON?

1 To get an idea of the size of the Moon in comparison to the Earth, use a small marble and a golf ball.

2 The diameter of the golf ball is roughly 4 cm. Cut a piece of

Marble (Moon)

The moon lander was 7 metres high. The top part took off to carry the astronauts back to the main spacecraft.

Backpacks had oxygen for breathing, as well as radios.

DO YOU KNOW

The Moon has no water and no wind. Footprints left by astronauts on its surface will never be worn away.

Helmets had gold-tinted visors to shield eyes from the Sun.

An umbrella-shaped antenna beamed pictures to Earth.

The astronauts were protected by thick, layered spacesuits.

string 30 times as long.

3 Put the golf ball (the Earth) at one end of the string. Stretch the string out and put the marble at the other end to see how far away the Moon is. It's roughly 30 times the Earth's diameter (12,713 km).

Golf ball (Earth)

A Moon car, called a lunar rover, was powered by batteries.

TV cameras took pictures of the desert-like landscape.

Why does the Moon change shape?

The Moon is lit by the Sun and doesn't give off any light of its own. However, the Sun only lights one half of the Moon, leaving the other half dark and invisible. We can only see one face or side of the Moon from Earth, and the Moon appears to change shape because we see this face from different angles during the $29\frac{1}{2}$ days the Moon takes to orbit the Earth. Sometimes the Sun lights all of the face of the Moon that we see. At other times only part is sunlit.

 DO YOU KNOW

The Moon spins once on its axis each time it goes round the Earth. This is why we just see one face of the Moon. Only space travellers have seen the other, far side of the Moon.

Over a month the Moon moves across the sky from west to east. Facing south, you'll see it change shape in the way shown below.

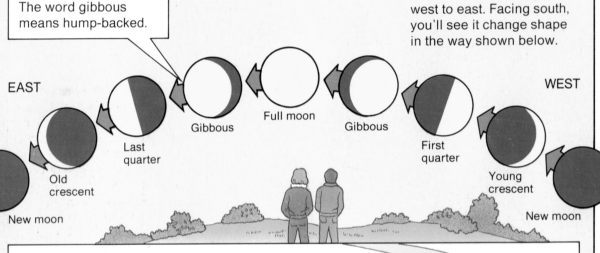

The word gibbous means hump-backed.

EAST

WEST

Gibbous

Full moon

Gibbous

Last quarter

First quarter

Old crescent

Young crescent

New moon

New moon

 MAKE A MOON SPINNER

The Moon is held in its orbit by the Earth's gravity, or pulling power. Without this, the Moon would fly off into Space. Here's a way to see how gravity acts.

1 Tie a length of string to a small plastic bucket. Make sure your knots are strong and that you have plenty of open space around you.

2 Whirl the bucket around. You'll feel a force tugging it outwards – only the string stops the bucket from flying off. The Earth's gravity is like the piece of string, holding the Moon in its orbit.

Why do eclipses happen?

There are two types of eclipse and they happen for different reasons. An eclipse of the Sun takes place if the Moon passes in front of the Sun. Sometimes the Moon blocks out the Sun completely and for a short time day becomes night. This is called a total eclipse. There are also eclipses of the Moon. These happen if the full moon passes through the Earth's shadow.

NEVER LOOK AT THE SUN

Never look directly at the Sun during an eclipse. It is just as dangerous to your eyes at these times as when it is shining normally.

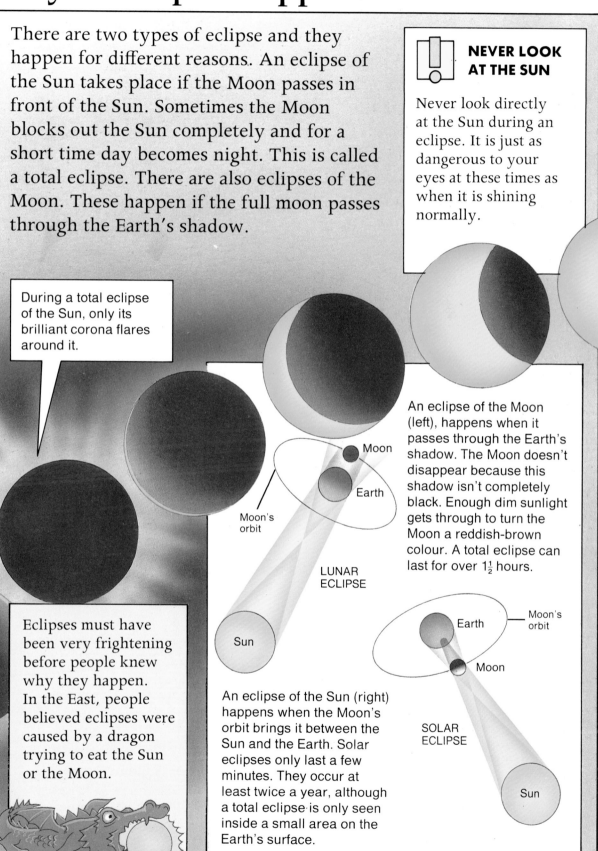

During a total eclipse of the Sun, only its brilliant corona flares around it.

Eclipses must have been very frightening before people knew why they happen. In the East, people believed eclipses were caused by a dragon trying to eat the Sun or the Moon.

Moon

Earth

Moon's orbit

LUNAR ECLIPSE

Sun

An eclipse of the Moon (left), happens when it passes through the Earth's shadow. The Moon doesn't disappear because this shadow isn't completely black. Enough dim sunlight gets through to turn the Moon a reddish-brown colour. A total eclipse can last for over $1\frac{1}{2}$ hours.

Earth

Moon's orbit

Moon

SOLAR ECLIPSE

Sun

An eclipse of the Sun (right) happens when the Moon's orbit brings it between the Sun and the Earth. Solar eclipses only last a few minutes. They occur at least twice a year, although a total eclipse is only seen inside a small area on the Earth's surface.

When did the Space Age begin?

The Space Age began on 4 October 1957, when the USSR launched Sputnik 1, the world's first artificial satellite. The first space flight by a person was on 12 April 1961. Yuri Gagarin, a Soviet cosmonaut, orbited the Earth once in the Vostok 1 spacecraft, proving that people could travel safely into Space and back again.

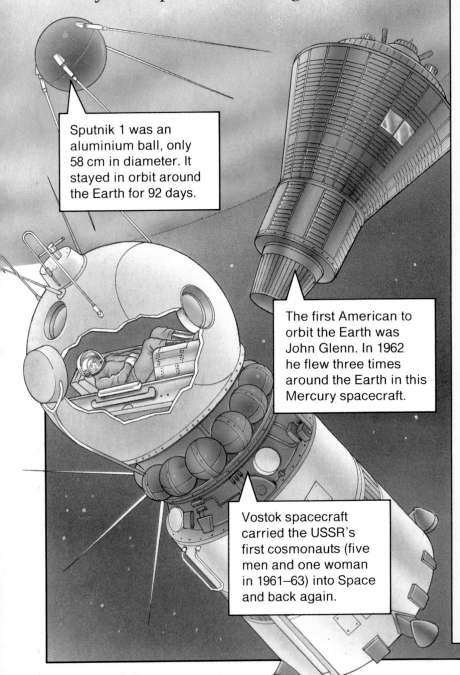

Sputnik 1 was an aluminium ball, only 58 cm in diameter. It stayed in orbit around the Earth for 92 days.

The first American to orbit the Earth was John Glenn. In 1962 he flew three times around the Earth in this Mercury spacecraft.

Vostok spacecraft carried the USSR's first cosmonauts (five men and one woman in 1961–63) into Space and back again.

 SPACE FACTS

● The first animal in Space was a dog called Laika. It was launched in 1957, in the USSR's Sputnik 2.

● The first TV pictures to be beamed across the Atlantic Ocean via a satellite were relayed by Telstar (USA).

● The first close-up pictures of the planet Mars were sent back to Earth in 1965, by the US spacecraft Mariner 4.

● The first spacecraft to fly round the Moon and land back on Earth was the USSR's Zond 5, in 1968.

● The first spacecraft to land on Mars were two US Viking probes (July and September 1976).

● The first spacecraft to visit the outer planets of the solar system was the USA's Voyager 2. It was launched in 1977 and flew past the planet Neptune in 1989.

When were space rockets invented?

The first space rockets were invented in the 1950s, but the Soviet scientist Konstantin Tsiolkovski (1857-1935) had realized how they would work much earlier. People began to test small rockets in the 1920s, and during World War II (1939-45) the Germans invented the V2 rocket, which was used as a weapon. After the war, scientists improved the V2's design until they made rockets powerful enough to travel into Space.

? DO YOU KNOW

Gunpowder firework rockets were invented in China, but no one knows when. They were known in Europe by the year 1241.

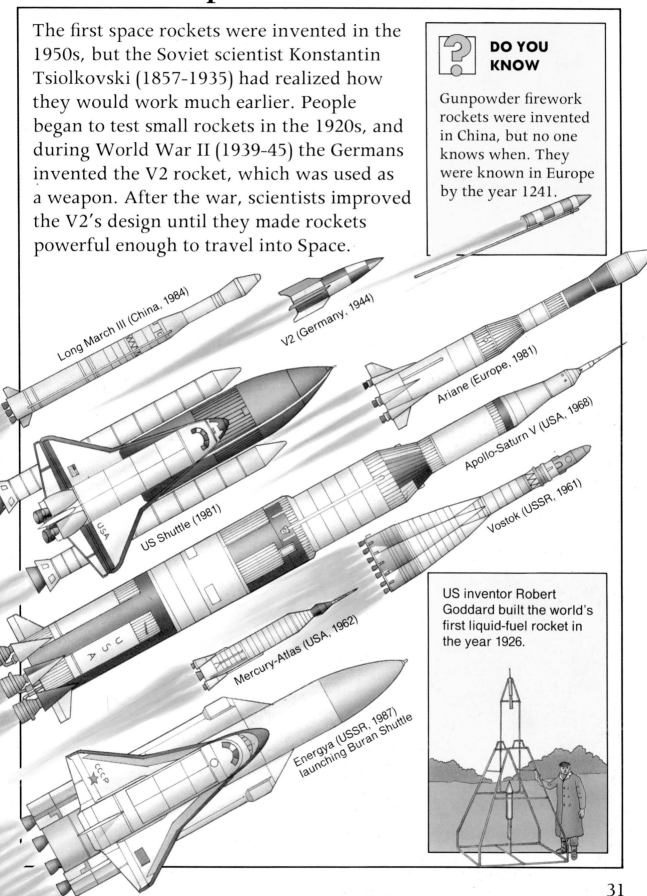

Long March III (China, 1984)

V2 (Germany, 1944)

Ariane (Europe, 1981)

Apollo-Saturn V (USA, 1968)

US Shuttle (1981)

Vostok (USSR, 1961)

Mercury-Atlas (USA, 1962)

Energya (USSR, 1987) launching Buran Shuttle

US inventor Robert Goddard built the world's first liquid-fuel rocket in the year 1926.

31

Who made the first spacewalk?

The cosmonaut Alexei Leonov was the first person to walk in Space. On 18 March 1965 he left his Voshkod 2 spacecraft and stayed outside for 24 minutes. A safety line made sure he didn't float away.

Since that time cosmonauts and astronauts have spent many hours working outside their spacecraft. Some have even been able to carry out important repairs to spacecraft while on spacewalks.

 DO YOU KNOW

The USA's John Young went into Space six times between 1965 and 1983. In 1981, he commanded the first flight of the shuttle Columbia.

Leonov floated outside Voskhod, weightless in Space. Without a safety line, he could have drifted away.

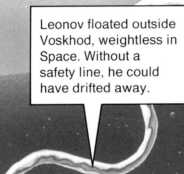

Nowadays US astronauts spacewalk wearing a special backpack called an MMU (manned maneouvring unit).

Astronauts move around by firing small gas jets on the base of the MMU.

Who was the first woman in Space?

The first spacewoman was Valentina Tereshkova (of the former USSR). She began training to be a cosmonaut in 1962, and on 16 June 1963 she was launched into Space in Vostok 6. She then spent more than two days orbiting the Earth.

DO YOU KNOW

The crews of the USA's Apollo and USSR's Soyuz spacecraft met up in Space in 1975.

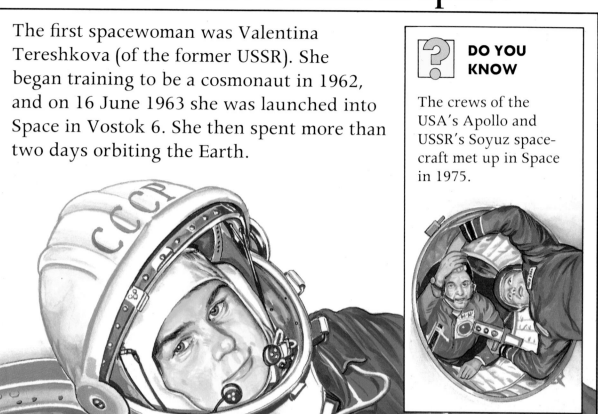

How long can people stay in Space?

Cosmonauts have lived for as long as a year on board space stations orbiting the Earth. Doctors study the effects of these long space flights on the cosmonauts' bodies, to make sure that they stay fit and well.

After 326 days in Space in 1987, Yuri Romanenko had grown taller, but his muscles were weaker.

Space stations have to get water and all their other supplies from Earth. The goods are sent up by spacecraft.

What is living in Space like?

Although today's space stations are not as big as the futuristic one shown here, life on board is still fairly comfortable. The biggest difference to living on Earth is that things are weightless in Space, so unless they are held or fixed down they just float about. This makes washing and eating rather tricky! Space travellers have to hold on to something or strap themselves down in order to stop drifting about.

Because things are weightless in Space, washing is difficult – water floats there, just like everything else. Space travellers have special showers, in which the water is vacuumed away so that no droplets can escape to float about.

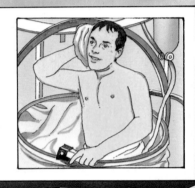

Space stations will be powered by solar panels, which collect the Sun's light and turn it into electricity.

Because of the special conditions in Space, scientists can do experiments that are impossible on Earth. They can make new alloys (mixtures of metals) and medicines. They also study how plants grow when weightless, and whether animals such as fish and spiders behave differently in Space.

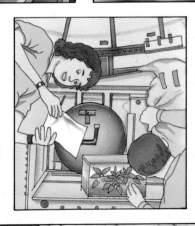

New crews and supplies will be ferried from Earth to the stations in spacecraft called shuttles.

Space tugs launched by rocket from Earth will bring bulky loads such as fuel and building materials.

New sections could be added to make the station bigger. In future, whole stations may be built in Space.

Shuttles will unload at docking ports with air-locks – special doors which stop air escaping into Space.

DO YOU KNOW

To stop their bodies weakening, space travellers have to exercise every day. They work out on special machines, but because of weightlessness they have to be strapped down to stop them floating away!

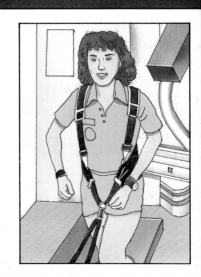

How did the Universe begin?

Nobody knows just how the Universe began, but we know that it is changing. All the millions of galaxies in the Universe seem to be speeding farther and farther apart – as though the Universe is expanding, or getting bigger. Because of this, many scientists think that at one time all the matter, or material, in the Universe was close together, and that a vast explosion sent it flying apart. Scientists call this explosion the Big Bang.

BALLOON UNIVERSE

1 Paint galaxy shapes close together all over a large balloon.

2 Let the paint dry, then blow up the balloon to see how the galaxies are moving apart as the Universe expands.

DO YOU KNOW

Quasars are the most distant objects that we know of in the Universe. They are huge bright galaxies very far away. The most distant known quasar is hurtling away at almost the speed of light – about 280,000 km a second! It is at least 6 billion light-years away, which means that the light now reaching Earth from this quasar began its journey towards us before the solar system existed!

2 About 1 billion years after the Big Bang, the first stars formed inside the developing galaxies.

1 The Universe may have started 10–20 billion years ago with the huge explosion that people call the Big Bang.

We live on a tiny planet close to a medium-sized star (the Sun), in one of millions of galaxies.

SATURN FACTS

- 1.4 billion km from the Sun
- 120,000 km in diameter
- 18 moons
- Atmosphere – hydrogen and helium gases
- One day lasts about 10.8 Earth hours

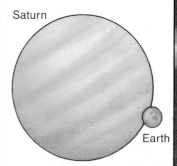

Saturn

Earth

3 The Universe is still expanding, as the galaxies carry on speeding apart. The Universe has no edge – there is always more Space ahead.

Will the Universe ever end?

Until we know more about how the Universe began, we can only guess whether it will ever end. If it did start with the Big Bang, the force of the explosion may be strong enough to keep the galaxies flying through Space forever. Then the Universe will never end. However, some scientists think that the galaxies might go into reverse and come closer together. Eventually they will crash into each other and the Universe will end in a Big Crunch.

URANUS FACTS

- 2.9 billion km from the Sun
- 51,000 km in diameter
- 15 moons
- Atmosphere – hydrogen, helium and methane gases
- One day lasts about 17 Earth hours

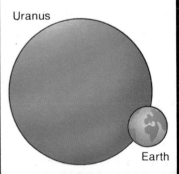

Uranus

Earth

1 Billions of years in the future, there may come a time when the galaxies' flight through Space slows down.

2 The galaxies would stop expanding and go into reverse. The Universe would then begin to shrink.

3 All the matter, or material, in the Universe may be squashed together in a Big Crunch.

Useful words

Asteroid   There are thousands of these mini-planets orbiting the Sun. Even the largest is much smaller than the Moon.

Astronomer   Someone who studies the stars.

Atmosphere   The layer of gases around a planet. The Earth's atmosphere is mainly nitrogen and oxygen gas. Mars and Venus have mainly carbon dioxide.

Axis   An imaginary line through the centre of planet. A planet spins on its axis.

Billion   One thousand million (1,000,000,000).

Comet   A huge cloud of gas and dust which orbits the Sun.

Constellation   A group of bright stars which make a pattern in the sky.

Core   The centre of a star or planet.

Corona   The outermost layer of the Sun. It looks like a faint halo and it stretches millions of kilometres into Space.

Cosmonaut   The Russian word for a space traveller.

Galaxy   A huge group of stars – even a small galaxy may contain several million stars. There are millions of galaxies in the Universe.

Gravity   Every object in the Universe has this pulling force. The Earth's gravity keeps our feet on the ground and stops us floating up into the air, for example, while the Sun's much stronger gravity keeps the Earth in its orbit and stops it flying off into Space.

Light-year   The distance a ray of light travels through Space in one year – about 9500 billion km. Distances in Space are measured in light-years.

Orbit   The curved path of something that travels around a star or a planet. Each planet, including Earth, has its own orbit around the Sun.

Satellite   Anything that orbits a planet. Moons are natural satellites. A spacecraft orbiting a planet is an artificial, or man-made, satellite.

The giant Saturn V rocket was the launch vehicle for the USA's Apollo programme.

Solar system   The Sun, the nine planets with their 50 or so moons, and the thousands of smaller bodies which also orbit the Sun.

Universe   The whole of Space and everything in it.

Index